The Karma Sutra

A Process of Liberation

Edward Pandemonium

© Copyright 2017 by Horngate Media, LLC

All rights reserved. No part of this book may be reproduced, transmitted, or utilized in any form or by any means, electronic or mechanical, including photocopying, recording, or by any information storage and retrieval system, without written permission from the author or publisher, except for brief quotations in critical articles, books, and reviews.

ISBN: 978-0-9909700-1-9

Book Layout & Pre-Press:
Philip H. Farber
http://www.hawkridgeproductions.com

Cover Design:
Fergal Fitzpatrick
http://www.fergalfitzpatrick.com

"Until you make the unconscious conscious, it will direct your life and you will call it fate." - C.G. Jung

CONTENTS

How (and Why) to Use This Course i

1. Preparing the Intellect 1
2. Cultivating Detachment and Will 7
3. Help from Your Own Guardian Spirit 27
4. The Source of Reality 37
5. The Crucial Importance of Ethics 49
6. Resolving Ancestral Karma 61
7. Working with Past Lives 69
8. The Cultivation of Daily Habitude 75
9. Merit, Service, Luck and Blessings 83

HOW (AND WHY) TO USE THIS COURSE

Karma is the most comprehensive, integral and holistic subject in the world - it is really the subject OF the world. It is TOTAL. Everything that exists and everything that happens is the result of Karma. Everything IS Karma. This is because Karma is the fabric of all causes and effects.

Pulling on a single thread can unravel a fabric. To unravel the karmic fabric of one Individual is to begin to pull at a single thread in the karmic fabric of the world. If more and more people work this course, that is more and more threads being pulled. Of course, even as the karmic fabric of either a life or a world is undone, a new one will be woven. That is just the way of things.

But we can become Creators rather than creatures. And if we can sort ourselves out, the world will be sorted out along the way.

This course draws upon concepts and ideas from world religions such as Hinduism, Buddhism and Jainism, but it must be emphatically stated that it is not meant to REPRESENT them. It is not meant to be traditional. The purpose of the course is to examine and engage with Karma from multiple angles so as to facilitate a unique experience of karmic intervention and hygiene.

There are nine lessons and the course is meant to be worked over nine months. You could easily spend a year on each lesson, but applying all of the approaches over the shorter time span creates a more impactful experience. Spending just a month on each lesson keeps you busy, helps to maintain momentum and has the benefit of symbolic analogy to a term of pregnancy. You can certainly work the course all over again after a few years or whenever you want to, and some of the practices are meant to become an ongoing part of your daily life. For added resonance, you might plan to either start or finish the course during your birth month.

At the beginning of each month, read the entire lesson through. The "Taking Action" section at the end will tell you how to apply the practices described in the lesson. As you apply the practices, take time every few days to re-read and think about the general information in the lesson. When the month is over, move on to the next lesson. Keep a journal to record your work with the exercises.

Each lesson is followed by several blank pages. These are provided for you to personalize the book by adding the highlights from your notes. Your insights, ideas, further questions, further answers and whatever else you wish to record can go on these pages.

Thank you for your decision to take on this work. It is a truly heroic endeavor and we are all cheering you on.

THE KARMA SUTRA

THE KARMA SUTRA

PREPARING THE INTELLECT

In approaching any subject, it is of the utmost importance to be as clear as possible on what can be done with the subject and what one personally hopes to do with the subject. While being as precise as possible is fundamentally expected in subjects like science and engineering, people tend to be much more sloppy when it comes to spiritual and psychological matters. This is a terrible mistake. Just as a muddled and sloppy approach to engineering can lead to exploding automobiles or collapsing bridges, a muddled and sloppy approach to spiritual and psychological issues can lead to explosions and collapses in all areas of existence.

WHAT KARMA IS

Our subject is Karma. Most people have heard of it. What goes around comes around. They will get what is coming to them. Pay it forward.

But how? Why? When? People talk about Karma but how many really know what it is? And of those truly concerned with it, how many really know what to do about it?

Our primary task in this first lesson is to create a clear, intellectual understanding of the subject of Karma. This will prepare you for the lessons to come but will also begin to have an effect on your Karma right now.

THE KARMA SUTRA

The concept of Karma comes from India. It is important in Hinduism, Buddhism, Sikhism, Jainism and even Daoism, as well as having diffused into popular thought around the world. The word derives from the proto-Indo-European root **kwer* that refers to doing or making. It contains the ideas of performing, accomplishing, causing, effecting, preparing and undertaking. There are similar concepts deriving from other cultures, but Karma is the best known to people today.

Karma is about causality. Causes produce effects, and those effects can provide the causes of other effects, on and on. This results in an incredibly complex web of processes. Where there is no consciousness, these processes are mechanical. Where there is consciousness, intention and agency become essential factors in opening a new dimension of Karma. You may have heard it said that thoughts become words and actions, which become habits, which become character, which becomes destiny. This will happen either way, but it can happen unconsciously or it can happen consciously.

TYPES OF KARMA

We can understand Karma more deeply by looking at some of its traditional categories and types. These include Sabija (or Sancita), Agami, Prarabdha, Kriyamana and the Jain distinction between Aghatiya and Ghatiya karmas.

The term *Sabija* means "with seed" and refers to a store of karmic patterns and potentials already within us at birth. These are acquired from the conditions of our conception, gestation and birth or even from previous lifetimes in traditional belief. These karmas are also called *Sancita*, which means "heaped together". Our basic genetic and epigenetic inheritance would be an example of Sabija or Sancita Karma.

The second main type is Agami Karma, where *Agami* means "approaching" and refers to karmic patterns that are acquired during life, mostly during childhood with later modifications. Agami karmas are the patterns of character and behavior that recur through our lives. These are the kinds of things which are, on one level, very familiar to us through psychology. Agami karmas roughly correspond to our conditioning and patterns in life.

The third main type is *Prarabdha*. The word means "commenced" or "begun" and this is already matured and manifesting Karma. It can not be cleared or changed as it is already happening, but we can control how we react to it and thus shape its ongoing results. These are effects from Sabija or Agami karmas that are already manifesting within our experience.

In another way, we might also look at Sabija as an archer's quiver of arrows, Agami as the arrow that is ready for shooting and Prarabdha as the arrow which has left the bow and can not return. Alternatively, Sabija might be thought of as the seed of a fruit tree and the potential for producing more fruit that is encoded within it, Agami as the tree and Prarabdha as the ripened fruits.

Our conscious agency and efforts are of vital importance in karmic processes. In reference to the metaphors above, consider the work in mastering archery and the choice in selecting targets; or the choice in whether to plant trees (and what kind) or to chop them down and make things from their wood. This relates to another important term tied to Agami Karma: *Kriyamana*, that which is "being made" by present actions.

It is further worth mentioning here the two main categories of Karma types within the Jain religion: *Ghatiya* karmas and *Aghatiya* karmas. Though we might disagree in some cases, the latter are considered to be "non-harming" to the soul and include the karmas that are responsible for the state of the body, mental capacity and birth status. The Ghatiya karmas, however, are considered to be "harming" to the soul by obscuring perception and knowledge and creating delusions and obstacles.

An interesting thing about even the Aghatiya karmas can be seen, though, if we use our bodies as an example. Today, we would see this in our genes. We know that our genes are the blueprint of our bodies, and so we might consider this a form of fixed Karma beyond our control. However, the science of epigenetics now tells us that factors in our environment, our diet and even our state of mind influence which genes get turned on and off and how they are expressed. So, while we already knew that our choices and actions can affect our bodies, we now know that they can do so as deeply as the genetic level. And those choices and actions can affect the genes of our children and even of their children.

In like fashion, the activities presented in this course work to alter the expression of our Karma.

CONSCIOUSNESS AND RESPONSIBILITY ARE KEY

The "soul-harming" karmas, though, are the primary concern in this course. As it is commonly expressed: Everything happens for a reason, but sometimes the reason is that you are stupid and make bad decisions. More gently put, the legendary psychologist Carl Jung said that when an inner situation is not made conscious, it appears outside of us as fate. That is what interests us here, ensuring that destiny is consciously Self-willed to the greatest possible extent rather than being thrust upon us by waves of external or mechanical forces.

Consciousness and Responsibility are key. We want to

highlight the distinction between unconscious compulsions and conscious efforts within the realm of Kriyamana - particularly its special applications through the lessons of this course to affect Karma as a whole.

TAKING ACTION

Find a place where you can be undisturbed for a half-hour or so to do this exercise. Once you do, start by asking yourself why you are sitting there doing the exercise now. Which is really three questions: What actions led you to be doing the exercise? Why are you doing it in this particular place? Why are you doing it at this particular time? Come up with as many reasons for each as you can.

When you answer those questions, question the answers. Why? What led to each thing? If you kept at this, you could go back to the begining of the universe with reasons.

Once you get good at the exercise, try it in many times and places and during mechanical activities. This will show you how Karma works and help you to begin thinking karmically.

NOTES

NOTES

NOTES

CULTIVATING DETACHMENT AND WILL

The first lesson of this course was intended to help you form a clear intellectual concept of Karma so that you might better understand the process ahead of you. This next lesson will help you to understand and cultivate the fundamental skills that you will need. Everything in this lesson will help to loosen your karmic bonds while also preparing you for the stages ahead.

The key themes in this lesson are Detachment and Will. These themes are complementary in that each helps in making the other progressively stronger. Cultivating detachment allows us to take a step back from things, so to speak, and helps to make us immune to unconscious reactions and the grip of karmic snares while also relaxing us on a deep level and granting peace of mind. Cultivating Will helps to give us greater conscious control over our actions and thus greater conscious control of the karmic effects that we generate.

For our purposes here, the cultivation of Detachment can be productively broken down into the practice of Dis-Identification and the handling of emotions as follows.

DIS-IDENTIFICATION

Much of our karmic burden is tied up in our identities,

the characters that we play. We have a lot of ideas about who we are and those ideas tell us how we should act and re-act in the world so as to "stay in character".

Dis-Identification is a psychological technique that works to distinguish and simplify our sense of Self by helping to dissolve our identification with our beliefs, thoughts, emotions and even our bodies. The secondary effect is that by doing so, it gives us greater control over those elements of our existence by establishing our perspective as a cause or creator over them rather than as an effect or creation of them.

You are the Experiencer. Anything that you perceive or experience is not you. It is something else.

The idea here is that you have a body and that your body is a very useful tool and enjoyable toy, but you are not your body. You have emotions and it is very easy to identify with your emotions when they are strong enough to overwhelm you, but they are not who you are. They are something very changeable that you experience. The same is true of your thoughts, ideas and beliefs. People can identify with these very strongly; but again, they are something that you experience, choose and create. Your core Self is that part of you that is pure Perception and Will. This part of you experiences and uses your mind, emotions and body as a collective vessel for existence and expression.

As a basic technique, verbally or mentally make an affirmation like the following:

"I have a body - but I am more than my body. I am my Self, the center, the one who is aware of my body. My body may be active or inactive. My body may be rested or tired, but I remain the same. I am the observer at the center of all of my experience. I am aware of my body, but I am more than my body.

"I have emotions - but I am more than my emotions. I

may feel calm or excited, but I recognize that I am not changing. I am aware of my emotions, but I am more than my emotions.

"I have an intellect - but I am more than my intellect. Whatever thoughts may come to me and regardless of how my beliefs have changed over the years, I remain the one who chooses and directs my thinking process. I am aware of the flow of my thoughts, but I am more than my thoughts.

"I am a center of pure consciousness. I am the Self."

As you do so, relax and allow yourself to enter a light trance state. Continue to distinguish between these elements and your core Self, the Observer. Redefine your body, emotions and mind as tools used by you.

Conceptually, feel yourself move up (or in) to a higher (or deeper) level of awareness. From this space and viewpoint, create a more transcendental concept of yourself by specifying the You who exists above and beyond the mundane character and circumstances. Represent this with a word or symbol that can function as an anchor for invoking the state again later (but realize that these anchors are also creations). Create an image of this Self as a stable center out of which you can live and express yourself.

This exercise can later be extended to include Dis-Identification from specific physical, emotional and intellectual elements as well as all mundane roles, jobs and tasks, relationships or incidents of personal history by making statements to the effect that while you may have experienced, done or believed some thing - currently or in the past - that thing does not permanently define you unless you want and allow it to.

MASTERING EMOTION

Emotion is a great karmic problem. Most adults are actually quite immature when it comes to their emotions. Emotionally speaking, it is as if they stopped growing at about the age of 10 or 11. Some of us have not even reached that far. Under these circumstances, with emotionally immature minds and relationships, how can we expect to attain our real potential in life? What of our societies? For most of us, our emotions seem to take over automatically, influencing how we think, how we behave and how we conduct our lives.

You can vastly increase your own personal power and create a happier, more harmonious life by gaining more conscious control over your emotional states. This will help you to stop many karmic reactions in their tracks and to stop generating new ones. Let us begin by taking a close look at how emotions work.

We usually think of our brain as a single organ, but this is not entirely accurate. Our brains consist of an interconnected conglomerate of several "sub-brains". The three major sub-brains correspond to periods of major evolutionary development, where new structures have simply been added onto already existing ones like the building of new structures onto an old house.

The most ancient of these three sub-brains is called the reptilian brain or the R-complex, which evolved around 200 million years ago. This primitive, reptile brain is basically a survival brain, possessing only a few ancient, pre-set "programs" to choose from. It is still influential in humans, performing in much the same way as it did for our remote ancestors by handling issues of basic survival, aggression and territoriality.

Next, the old mammalian brain, or limbic system, is about 60 million years old and is sandwiched between the R-complex and the new mammalian brain. The limbic system contains a much greater number of programs than its predecessor, allowing it a far wider range of response. In fact, we could call it our "emotion brain" as it plays a major part in the generation of our emotions.

For example, it has been found that the amygdala, a small almond-shaped structure located in the limbic system, plays a major role in both aggression and fear. If the amygdala of a placid, domestic animal is stimulated electrically, the animal will be roused into a state of great fear or frenzy. If the amygdala of a naturally ferocious animal is surgically removed, it becomes docile and will even tolerate being stroked.

Finally, the newest sub-brain is the new mammalian brain or neocortex, and has only been around for a few million years. In humans, the neocortex is also the largest of the three sub-brains and accounts for about five-sixths of the brain's entire size. The role of the neocortex is very important in relationship to the other two sub-brains and is the key to the work of mastering our emotions. The function of the neocortex is to detect patterns and interpret the "meanings" of situations.

For example, in order for you to react to something with fear, you must perceive or interpret that situation as warranting a fearful response. The programs of the R-complex and limbic system are hard-wired and their emotional responses are not always appropriate to our life experiences as modern humans. With work, the neocortex enables us to master those responses.

Emotions involve the human brain at all levels. Generally speaking, the oldest sub-brain activates the physical response, based on orders from the middle sub-brain, which is based upon the analysis of the situation that the newest sub-brain provides. However, the new sub-brain does not always win. It can be temporarily shunted out of decision-making as older and simpler circuits take over. We will call this process "downshifting".

When we downshift, full use of our new sub-brain is suspended and more control is given to our lower brains. These older, simpler sub-brains are...well, older and simpler. With the downshift, there is a corresponding loss of intelligence that can often lead to real problems. Our thinking, if it can be called such under these circumstances, becomes muddled and less conscious.

Of course, in the kind of life-threatening situations where we literally have to fight or run, we are required to take immediate action. The lower sub-brains evolved over millions of years to work well in these kinds of situations. They were designed to make quick decisions. For this reason, downshifting happens as a reflex mechanism.

The obvious problem, though, is that most of our emotional experiences are not actually on this survival imperative level. When we continue to downshift when it is not necessary or even beneficial to do so, our ability to think straight seems to vanish and our ability to properly handle situations goes with it. The man or woman that is acting solely under the influence of these older sub-brains is, literally, acting like an animal.

However, by learning how to counteract or prevent this from happening, we can greatly increase our personal power and our control over our emotions. This goes to the heart of the problem of emotional control. Getting a handle on our emotions is a matter of gaining more conscious control over those behaviors which ordinarily engage automatically without conscious thought.

In most instances, our negative emotional responses are directly preceded by automatic thoughts, which remain hidden for most of us. Unless you train yourself to look for these thoughts, you will probably not be aware of them. But once you do learn how to catch hold of your automatic thoughts, you will not only become aware of them but will also learn how to control them. Learning how to identify your automatic thoughts is one of the most critical aspects of gaining more emotional control.

By changing the way you think, you can change the way you feel and act. Most of our emotions are a result of the interpretations we make of the events around us. This is quite different from the way we normally think about our emotional states. Usually, we tend to regard our emotional responses as being directly caused by outside events and situations. This view is reflected in the way we talk. For example, we say that someone made us angry or sad. However, it is not the events and situations that cause emotional reactions, but our interpretation of the event which triggers the emotional response. Once we grasp this, we can see that it is of enormous importance for emotional control.

Consider this sequence:

EVENT - INTERPRETATION - EMOTION - (RE)ACTION

For the most part, we are unaware of this process of interpretation or assigning meaning to events and situations because it happens automatically and very rapidly. It is this ability of the mind to interpret events quickly and automatically that leads to the false perception that other people and outside events generate emotions. However, the reality is that it is the meaning that we assign to people and events that actually generates emotions.

The meaning that we assign to our experiences is based on patterns of thinking that are so automatic and rapid that we usually do not even notice them. It is kind of like wearing glasses. After wearing them for a while, we tend to forget that they are there. However, even though we have forgotten them, they are stil there and influence our perception. Some of our patterns of thought are like glasses with scratched and dirty lenses.

And because the interpretation phase of the sequence above is so automatic, we mistakenly perceive the sequence as only:

EVENT - EMOTION - (RE)ACTION

Terrible mistake!

However, once you learn that your emotional responses are preceded by automatic thoughts and interpretations, it is not difficult to train yourself to be aware of them during various events and circumstances. An exercise will be provided below that will help you to do this. The first step is to know that you need to start looking for them. All that you need is that knowledge and the power of Will that you will also begin to cultivate in this lesson.

Another problem issue is identification, which we have already looked at but which deserves further mention here. Identification with emotional states is shown by thoughts or statements such as "I am angry" or "I am sad" rather than "I feel angry" or "I feel sad". This may seem like hairsplitting, but it really is an essentially important distinction. When we identify ourselves with our emotional states, it is difficult to control them and we open up the possibility (and probability) that we will become dominated by them.

The secret of emotional control is to disengage yourself from emotional states, to pull back and cease identifying with your feelings and moods. This does NOT mean suppressing your feelings. It means recognizing that they are something that you are experiencing in relation to events and not as your identity. The examples that we have used such as anger or sadness are the kinds of emotions that usually cause us the most trouble but this also applies to our positive emotions. Our happiness can also lead us astray if we lose our perspective of what it is and how it is created, internally by our own thinking and not by other people or outside conditions.

Emotional issues can be very complicated but we have a few key methods that can help us to get right to the heart of managing them.

The first method for mastering emotion is to look to your physical state. Lack of sleep or poor nutrition can increase stress and result in irritability or depressed moods. These are issues that affect many people, so making sure that you get enough rest and making some simple dietary changes can perhaps take a lot of the edge off.

Another powerful method for learning emotional control is to train yourself in the ability to take a step back from your emotional reactions. How many times have you found yourself swept up in a tide of emotion, only to later wish that you had called a "time-out" before you made a decision or took a certain action? Doing so is a learnable skill that only requires the will to do so and the perseverance to make it a habitual behavior. The process is as follows:

1. Recognize your stressful feelings and make the decision to call a "time-out" before they escalate. The key skill in this first step is to realize that you are feeling stressed and that you need to disengage before you get swept up in the situation and allow your emotions to take control of you. In a sense, this step is like pressing the pause button while watching television.

2. Shift your focus away from your racing thoughts and emotions. Focus your attention instead on the area around your heart and for about ten seconds or so, imagine that you are breathing in and out "through" your heart. Try to keep your breath slow and even. This will direct your attention away from your thoughts and

emotions while also (at least somewhat) relaxing you. This will enable you to quickly gain a more clear-headed perspective, allowing you to consider appropriate ways of handling your current situation.

3. Ask your heart for an appropriate response to the current situation. The answer will come from your intuition or source of common sense. We are all in possession of vast sources of intelligence and creativity and need only open ourselves up to them. Open yourself up and listen to the answer that your heart gives you.

As you practice this technique more and more, it will start to become second nature to you. After a while, you will no longer need to think about the steps involved but will start to do them automatically. Mastering this technique will provide you with increased emotional control, enabling you to maintain inner poise and giving your mind more clarity. It will greatly improve your ability to communicate with others and to bring more quality to your relationships. In general, it will help you to take back control of your life by eliminating knee-jerk reactions. Because of the effects that our emotional states have upon our bodies, you may also enjoy greater health and physical well-being.

Finally, another important aspect of emotional control is the ability to handle what might be described as "mood contagion". We can often become "infected" by the emotions and moods of others. You can catch both negative and positive emotions alike. We have probably all had the experience of feeling rather solemn and serious and then encountering someone who is in a cheerful mood...or the other way around. Usually, that other person's mood rubs off onto us and we find our own emotional tone rising or falling accordingly.

So, emotional control is not only a matter of managing your own emotions but also of dealing with other people's contagious moods.

Begin paying attention to how you feel around different people. Do you feel sad around some people and happy around others? Examine your emotional responses. Ask yourself whether the feeling is your own or if you might have caught it from someone else. By observing how you feel both before and after interacting with various people, you will begin to see how other people's emotions may spread to you. Simply recognizing that an emotion actually belongs to (originated with) someone else may be enough to prevent the mood from spreading to you. Basically, protecting yourself from emotional contagion is a matter of monitoring your own engagement and not allowing yourself to become contaminated with other people's negativity.

This has been a long section in a long lesson, detailing a complex issue and process. The steps to mastering this material are, however, quite simple to follow.

1. Continue to study this material to gain understanding of how emotions work and what can be done to manage them.

2. Make sure that you get enough rest and proper nutrition so that physical deficiencies do not aggravate your stress levels and affect your moods.

3. Begin practicing the technique for calling a "time-out" on your emotional responses.

4. Start monitoring yourself for mood contagion.

If you follow these steps with sincerity and seriousness, you will be well on your way to achieving emotional control.

As with so many of the issues that we are working with in this course, the mastery of our emotional states is also about restoring our personal power.

Most people believe that external circumstances are the driving force of their lives. This passive orientation towards life leads to the feeling that we are victims of circumstance or fate. We tend to get so used to things happening to us that we forget that we can control our own lives. This is especially relevant to our emotions.

When we allow ourselves to be overwhelmed by anger, sadness or other emotional states, we are no longer in control of ourselves. Furthermore, we tend to lose our ability to think clearly when our consciousness is flooded with emotions. Consider that humans typically use only a tiny fraction of their potential. A big part of that problem is that we waste so much of our time getting bogged down by our own emotions. We encounter various problems and difficulties and find ourselves shrinking away from life, exaggerating the importance of present difficulties. We seldom feel relaxed and healthy enough to take a clear, objective view of our own lives, and so are usually functioning far below our proper level of effectiveness.

However, we do not have to be to be at the mercy of our moods and feelings. We can learn to control them. By taking control of our emotions and minimizing the degree to which we indulge in negative emotions, we both increase our personal freedom and become vastly more effective and efficient human beings.

CULTIVATING WILL

Along with the receptive power of Perception, the active power of the Will is the function that is most basic and fundamentally related to the Self. Active existence as a Self is experienced as the volitional power to act on our own intentions and initiative.

The natural world is unconscious and mechanical. Everything is the effect of something else. Likewise, society is also largely unconscious and mechanical.

People simply react to things more often than they act with true consciousness. We all do this to some extent. We let ourselves be carried along by events and we react to whatever happens to us without thinking. We do what we do because of what the other person did. In this way, many people live their entire lives like puppets, with their strings all tangled up with everyone else's.

However, you do have the choice to be a true Cause. Should you choose to exercise them, you possess the powers of Self-determinism: the power to reason, the power to imagine and the volitional power to act on the results of your reasoning and imagining. In every moment, the possible choices of how you might use these powers are practically infinite. Who and what you become is ultimately the result of your own choices through either the exercise or neglect of your own powers of choice and intention. Even if you allow others to make the decisions for you or if you simply throw the decisions to chance, that is still your decision. It is ultimately your Will and Desire that generate your power to act and everything that you are. To function freely and not be compelled by external forces results from the conscious, intelligent and regular exercise of Will.

How effective is your Will? Ask yourself the following questions and really think about them. Look closely at your life and relationships, and be honest with yourself. Record your answers.

Do you allow other people to control you?

Do you allow your emotions to get the better of you?

Are you restricted by your habits?

Do you doubt yourself?

Are you lazy or easily distracted?

Do you know what you really want? If so, do you act on it?

Once you have considered and answered these questions, the following actions will help to strengthen your Will. Compare what the questions above have taught you about yourself with the opportunities for change that these actions provide. Begin by doing any one of these things every day for a week. Then, do any three of these things every day for another week. Many opportunities will appear if you watch for them. Record your experiences in your journal.

Do something that you do not want to do but that needs to be done.

Do something that you have never done before.

Do something that you do regularly in a different way.

Break a bad habit.

Make a plan or a promise and follow through on it.

Refrain from saying something that you are tempted to say, but should not.

Say something that you do not want to say, but should.

Finally, with regard to the exercise of making a plan or promise and then following through on it, you might make a promise to yourself to follow the entire program laid out in this course to the end. Should you follow through on that promise, even if you gain nothing else from this work, you will at least know that your Will has been tried and proven. However, should you truly master this program, you will find that each part of the process supports all of the others and that EVERYTHING is material for work and an opportunity to gain further strength.

TAKING ACTION

1. Start with the basic Dis-Identification exercise as a daily practice for a week or until you get the feel of it.

2. Meanwhile make sure that you get proper nutrition and rest and start checking yourself for mood contagion. As you get used to paying attention to your moods, incorporate the "time out" process as an extension of emotional Dis-Identification.

3. As the other exercises become familiar - say in the second week or around the middle of the month - ask yourself the questions about your Will and begin incorporating the Will-strengthening practices. As said, begin by doing any one of these things every day for a week. Then, do any three of these things every day for another week.

4. As an advanced exercise, try applying the Dis-Identification exercise to the following roles as they apply to you:

Nationality

Son/Daughter

Husband/Wife (or equivalent)

Mother/Father

Religious Label

Political Label

Job Title

Other Group Member (list all that apply)

What does being each of these things mean to you? Record your answers. How much of what being these things means to you have you defined for yourself, how much have you agreed with and how much have you merely accepted? Record those answers, too. Then, try to dis-identify with all of it, assuming the detached position of the Self and viewing all these as things that you can "put on" or "take off" as you will.

You could go even further still with this by describing yourself as fully as possible from your own point of view, listing your various qualities (good and bad) and subjecting them to the same questions and process.

5. Finally, here is an advanced exercise in acting from the detached perspective of the Experiencer or Observer. First, simply read this lesson. You could read anything, really, but the lesson is here and its content may help. Just read it. Next, read it again but take a mental step backward and *observe* yourself reading it. Try that a few times until you get a handle on it. After reading the same text several times, your mind might start to wander. Do not let it, be deliberate. Once you are good at this, read the lesson again, observing yourself reading and simultaneously observing your breathing. Your detached Self should be observing both the part of your mind that is reading and the part of your body that is breathing. You may notice some strange sensations. Record your experiences.

Any progress that you make with this exercise will be very beneficial for you. Of course, you can also take it further by observing other activities (perhaps not driving) while also observing your breathing.

NOTES

NOTES

HELP FROM YOUR OWN GUARDIAN SPIRIT

This course is intended to engage all aspects of your being. That being so, this lesson is a little different than the previous two and advocates more overtly spiritual (or symbolic) practices. This does not make them any more (or less) important or effective than the others, it just means that they are meant to engage more of your being.

YOUR GUARDIAN SPIRIT

You have a powerful ally in working with your Karma: your Guardian Spirit. Everyone has their own unique Guardian Spirit. Your Guardian Spirit is a messenger that seeks to remind you of your pure and true nature and to help you to get back to that state of being.

Many cultures and religions describe these Spirits by different names and in different ways. If there is one that you identify with, you can adapt the material in this lesson to the practices that are appropriate to your own religion or culture. Otherwise, you can simply think of the Guardian Spirit as the highest and best part of yourself.

In a sense, your Guardian Spirit is understandable as an ideal parent with both fatherly and motherly qualities. Your Guardian Spirit knows all about you, intimately, and understands and supports you totally. It is an ever-present guide and mentor. It is also the hidden manifester of the plans and patterns that make up your reality.

It is widely believed that Guardian Spirits also comprise their own society within their own realm of existence and that they are all in communication with each other, weaving their plans and patterns together on that level of reality. More people becoming aligned on the human level with their own Guardian Spirits would better facilitate the manifestation of these plans and patterns upon the Earth.

The Guardian Spirit is especially concerned with the fulfillment of your personal meta-needs. Meta-needs are needs for nourishment and growth that go beyond the ordinary, physical, emotional and intellectual needs of life. It is concerned with the special needs that make life meaningful and extraordinary.

Some essential meta-needs are Self-actualization, Self-sufficiency and Wholeness, Truth and Meaning, Beauty, Perfection and Uniqueness, Goodness and Justice, Aliveness, Power and Freedom. If you earnestly seek understanding and fulfillment of these needs, your Guardian Spirit will be happy and will respond.

Guardian Spirits are also frequently associated symbolically with birds or winged beings and it may be profitable to include this symbolism when invoking your own Guardian Spirit below. The home-center of the Guardian Spirit is often perceived as being slightly above the top of the head, though sometimes it is perceived within the heart.

CONTACTING YOUR GUARDIAN SPIRIT

The basic process for contacting your Guardian Spirit and starting to develop a more conscious relationship with it is as follows, but may be further enhanced and solemnized as you will. Even in the absence of traditional practices, many people find candles, incense and uplifting music to be nice additions that help to make the occasion special.

Will to contact your Guardian Spirit and ask for it to reveal itself and to help in your life. Proclaim "May I Awaken and be whole".

Take several slow, deep, easy breaths while imagining and willing that your body is filling up with power. Continue to do this while focusing your attention on the space just above your head. When the energy has built up into a powerful charge, look straight up into the space above your head and blow upward in one full exhalation, sending the accumulated power, via the breath, to the Guardian Spirit.

Speak thus to your Guardian Spirit: "Guardian Spirit, who are you and what is your Will? I would know the Mystery of my Self."

Take a slow, deep breath and relax. After a moment, you will likely feel a return flow from your Guardian Spirit. This often feels like a fluid pouring down upon your head and flowing down over you. It is thus a tradition to say: "Let the rain of blessings fall". Be open and receptive to the experience and mindful of it.

STRENGTHENING THE CONNECTION

After you have done this basic invocation a few times

and become used to it, the process can be enhanced as follows. Relax and focus your attention on your Heart. This means your actual, physical heart but also the core of being that the physical organ often symbolizes. Breathe in and out "through" the Heart for a moment. Then, meditate upon one of the meta-needs below and call it up within your Heart.

Self-actualization
Self-sufficiency
Wholeness
Truth
Meaning
Beauty
Perfection
Uniqueness
Goodness
Justice
Aliveness
Power
Freedom

Get the feeling of the quality and keep it flowing for a few minutes and then mentally send the feeling to parts of yourself and/or to others as feels right. If the experience feels either blocked or overwhelming, simply relax. Do not try to either force it or restrict it. When you feel that the process has reached its conclusion, write down any insights that you may have experienced.

This process helps to conduct these qualities into the human personality and anchor them within it, strengthening the connection with your Guardian Spirit.

INVOKING THE AID OF YOUR GUARDIAN SPIRIT FOR CHANGE

You are always connected to your Guardian Spirit, who loves you and will always help you with requests that are in line with the goal of returning to your true nature and fulfilling the meta-needs described above.

So, of course, your Guardian Spirit will certainly be happy and ready to help with your Karma. Your Guardian Spirit is like a hawk or eagle that flies high over the world. It sees and knows about many things that are hidden within us and around us. The process for focusing on an issue and invoking the aid of the Guardian Spirit is quite simple.

1. Invoke your Guardian Spirit as you have previously done. The Guardian Spirit may also give you new methods of communication by inspiring ideas or leading you to information. If this happens, adopt those methods. Otherwise, the basic method is still perfectly good.

2. Focus on what you want to change. At first, you may state something very general, such as: "I want to be relieved of my karmic errors and burdens, so that my spirit, mind, body and life may be liberated and healed in all ways."

Your Guardian Spirit fully understands your condition, all of its causes and how to resolve problems and improve it. You do not have to worry about trying to figure all of that out for yourself right now. You will be thinking of those things later but will have the support of your Guardian Spirit's inspiration.

You will also later become aware of more specific issues that you can then focus upon with this process.

3. Tell yourself, out loud, that it is alright to change. You might say something like: "I know and agree that this change is necessary and good, and I allow myself to experience this liberation and healing with the help of my Guardian Spirit."

4. Thank your Guardian Spirit for assistance. Allow your Guardian Spirit to do its work and notice when changes occur. Be ready to help it by also noticing when further inspirations, insights and opportunities for change appear.

A PURIFICATION RITUAL

The following small rite complements the emotional work from the previous lesson and can help to clear karmic complexes that are held together by knotted-up emotional energy. While such knots or blocks may be entirely unknown to conscious awareness, they can strongly affect us unconsciously.

The only thing that you will need is a large glass of pure water and perhaps a candle to represent the presence of your Guardian Spirit. Invoke the aid of your Guardian Spirit for change as described above.

Breathe calmly and deeply, expanding your abdomen as you inhale and letting it relax as you exhale. As you do so, imagine the breath filling you with life energy. When you feel saturated with this energy, exhale, projecting the life energy through your hands and breath into the water.

Return to your special breathing and fill yourself with life energy again. When you are again filled with this energy, create a clear picture or feeling in your mind of being completely, perfectly clean and clear in spirit, mind, heart and body. Within and without. Once you have it, look up into the home-center of your Guardian Spirit - the space above your head - and send the image or feeling and the life energy to your Guardian Spirit by quickly blowing upward in one full exhalation.

It may be immediate or may take a moment, but when you feel energy beginning to return from your Guardian Spirit, direct it into the glass as you did before. Then drink the whole glass of charged water immediately and feel the sensations of the energy flowing throughout your entire body, leaving you feeling light, clean, and energized.

Thank your Guardian Spirit, clap your hands three times, proclaim that it is done and go about your other activities.

TAKING ACTION

As always, record your experiences with all of these actions.

1. Spend one week doing the simple exercise for contacting your Guardian Spirit as a daily practice.

2. Spend a second week invoking the qualities associated with meta-needs into your Heart as a daily practice. Try out different ones but use only one per session.

3. Spend a third week invoking help for change as described above. Again, do this daily. Ask for general help with your Karma as described but feel free to add any specific karmic issues that you wish - but only one per session.

4. Now, you will have built up quite a bit of momentum.

Spend the last week doing the purification ritual as a daily practice.

5. AFTER you have done all of this, start looking into the subject of Self-Talk and the use of technologies such as Hypnosis or Neurolinguistic Programming for clearing out deeper psychological patterns. The momentum that you have built will help you in finding what you need.

NOTES

NOTES

THE SOURCE OF REALITY

When we worked with Dis-Identification in Lesson Two, we were trying to start shifting our attention out of the habit of identifying with mutable, karmic aspects and elements of being and back into our true, essential, core Self. In terms of subject and object, this Self is the essential Subject, the singular - indeed, monadic - point of awareness and intention. Everything else that we might have previously thought of as "I" or "me" or "myself" is simply a collection of objects of our awareness with which we have identified. This includes our mind and thoughts, our emotions, our body, our name and all of the roles that we play in life.

LAYERS OF EXISTENCE

So, if we understand ourselves as being fundamentally just points or essential "sparks" with the basic powers of Perception and Will, then we understand that each one of us is the perceptual and intentional center of our own experiential universe. That experiential universe proceeds outward from us in rings or layers of immediacy and intensity of engagement.

First are those things already mentioned that we commonly identify with and think of as who we are: mind, emotions, body and so on. This is the character or persona that we create and maintain for ourselves. Next might come our lovers, family, friends and other intimates. After that might come the people that we work with, organizations that we belong to, our religion, our ethnicity or nationality and any other social or cultural groups. Then might come humanity as a species, followed by the totality of nature, the whole cosmos and so on.

HOW YOU CREATE YOUR LIFE

Essentially, though, we are really just that spark amidst a vast soup of energies. That is the basic truth. However, we engage with that soup and create meaning from it by means of our biological senses and then by identification and belief. As said, our experience of existence is organized into those rings or layers described above and we then define and create our personal worlds of experience within them. Our identity progressively defines our beliefs, which progressively defines our identity in a circular process. Usually unconsciously, we are attracted to beliefs that support our identifications and we define our identity by what we believe. Generally speaking, any statement that involves the words "because" or "should" will fit into this category.

Your personal history and the narrative that you tell yourself about it, your favorite music, the people that you are attracted to, the jokes that you find funny, the work that you do, your political opinions, your religious affiliation or lack thereof, your philosophy of life and code of right and wrong - all of these generate various karmas when expressed as action, and they are all the result of your identifications and beliefs.

EXPERIENCING REALITY

Here is an exercise.

Name something in your past that gave you an advantage that you enjoy today. What made that advantageous? When did you first encounter the idea that such a thing was an advantage and why did you agree with that?

Likewise, name something in your past that gave you a disadvantage or problem today. What made that disadvantageous? When did you first encounter the idea that such a thing was a problem and why did you agree with that?

Come up with about three examples of each and record them. Contrary to the basic instructions, do this now before reading any more of this lesson.

Now read this story.

An old Chinese farmer had a mare that broke through the fence and ran away. When his neighbors learned of it, they came to the farmer and said, "What bad luck this is. You don't have a horse during planting season." The farmer listened and then replied, "Bad luck, good luck. Who knows?"

A few days later, the mare returned with two stallions. When the neighbors learned of it, they visited the farmer. "You are now a rich man. What good fortune this is," they said. The farmer listened and again replied, "Good fortune, bad fortune. Who knows?"

Later that day, the farmer's only son was thrown from one of the stallions and broke his leg. When the neighbors heard about it, they came to the farmer. "It is planting season and now there is no one to help you," they said. "This is truly bad luck." The farmer listened, and once more he said, "Bad luck, good luck. Who knows?"

The very next day, the Emperor's army rode into the town and conscripted the eldest son in every family. Only the farmer's son with his broken leg remained behind. Soon the neighbors arrived. Tearfully, they said, "Yours is the only son who was not taken from his family and sent to war. What good fortune this is..."

Now, with this story in mind, go back to your own examples and consider how each of the advantages might also be or could have become a disadvantage. Likewise, consider how each problem might also be or could become an advantage or breakthrough. Record these, then contemplate how the best might be made of any situation and also record your thoughts on that.

PERCEPTUAL FILTERS

In this lesson, we are primarily concerned with that concept of you as a pure spark of awareness and intention within a vast sea of energies and we want to get back to that experience as best as we can. This means getting back as best as possible to pure experience of things without our usual perceptual filters (identification, beliefs, thoughts and so on). It may be very difficult to remove these filters completely but we can certainly learn to diminish them with some relatively simple exercises.

Here, it would be good to experiment with simple perception of things. A list of them will be provided below. Observe the thing. Define its outer boundaries and get a fix on the space it occupies. Feel its weight, notice its color and check out its other characteristics. Observe the thing without thinking about it or interacting with it. See if you can temporarily merge with or become it in your attention.

Here is a good order for items to use in practicing this exercise.

1. Simple objects such as rocks or small, simple manmade objects. As you progress, move up to larger things like buildings or small bodies of water.

2. Plants and animals.

3. Individual people. Practice with a variety of sexes, ages and types. Then try groups of people, trying to get a sense of their prevailing moods, attitudes or belief systems.

4. The world as a whole. You might take this in layers, starting with all humans, then all plants and animals, then the geological mass of the planet.

5. Bodies of knowledge and belief systems. These might include sciences, political ideologies, religious beliefs and even advertising campaigns. Experience these as "objects" as with the others, though these are "objects" within our minds. Start with some that you like, then some that you do not care about and then some that you

might find unpleasant. Just try to experience the feeling of these while remaining as neutral as possible without your mind getting into a lot of thoughts and words.

6. Your own beliefs as you continue to uncover them.

One way to reveal your beliefs is to use affirmations. You are probably familiar with the use of these simple, positive statements to affirm what we want in our lives. A twist on this practice is to make the affirmations and pay attention to any doubts, disagreements, counterpoints or even any reluctance to do the exercise that may come up. A list of affirmations will be provided below that you can use to do this. Record everything that comes up for use with this exercise and the important clearing exercise given later.

Here are some affirmations:

I know what I want. / I do not know what I want.

I have what I need. / I need something.

I enjoy my body. / My body is a problem.

My past does not exist. / My past is always here.

I appreciate what I see.

I own what I experience.

I am right here. / I do not know where I am.

I know what to do. / I do not know what to do.

I do what I want. / I can not do what I want.

I know how to do it. / I do not know.

I am relaxed.

Everything I see is illusion. / Everything I see is real.

My mind is quiet.

I am happy being who I am. / I want to be someone else.

I know myself. / I wonder who I am.

I am not a victim. / I feel like a victim.

I am unique.

I am the source of it all.

That should give you plenty to work with as far as your beliefs go. If you want go deeper into this in the future, you can use affirmations that you like or look for more that deal with specific issues or themes.

After you get good at this perceiving exercise, you can stop being neutral and intentionally project moods or opinions onto the thing that you are perceiving. Use opposites like "good" / "bad", "beautiful" / "ugly", "precious" / "worthless" and so on, going back and forth multiple times. Run through several in sequence. Always go back to neutrality at the end, though. Run through the above types of things (from rocks to beliefs) again, doing this as a second exercise. This will strengthen your control of your experiences by making them less automatic and reactive. And, the more responsibility or ownership that we take for conditions around us, the more empowered we become.

THOUGHTFORMS

Again, you are a spark of pure existence in a sea of energies. All of these things that we have talked about are things that you project onto reality and that define and filter your experience. So, here is perhaps the simplest method of all for uncovering beliefs. We showed in Lesson Two that emotions are reactions to *interpretations* of events and not to the events themselves. If you are experiencing a particular feeling, then, you might just ask yourself why you feel that way. When your mind says "I feel this way *because*....", remember what we said about "because" indicating a belief. You will start to uncover beliefs. Take the "becauses" and keep asking why and you will come to understand the belief underlying the feeling - the belief that creates the feeling.

The beliefs and psychological identifications that we keep talking about collect energies such as emotion and effort and form clusters or bubbles of information and fixed energy around themselves. Buddhists, among others, talk about these clusters or bubbles as *thoughtforms* and would say that all of experienced reality is made up of various thoughtforms.

Now, if you are not Buddhist or similarly inclined, you may be skeptical. However, consider that thoughts and emotions can be measured by machines. Moreover, something like thoughtforms certainly underlie all group efforts, cultures or societies; and at least all manmade objects are the tangible manifestation of something like a thoughtform. So, within the realm of existence that we are proposing for thoughtforms to exist, distinctions between plain description and metaphor are somewhat meaningless.

Rather than the general sea of energies that we have mentioned, we are actually experiencing reality through a collection of perceptual bubbles, blobs or force fields of energy and information within that sea. This, in itself, is not necessarily a bad thing. An endless sea of undifferentiated potential would become quite dull. What IS a bad thing is when these processes become unconscious, automatic and outside of our control. As your awareness drifts into and out of different bubbles, they may compulsively trigger various thoughts, feelings and behaviors.

CHANGING REALITY

In closing, here is a process that uses everything from this lesson to create possibilities for deep change.

1. Focus on a thoughtform from your collection and observe it with basic perception as described above. Define its outer boundaries and get a fix on the space it occupies. Feel its weight (if any), notice its color (if any) and check out its other characteristics. Observe the thing without thinking about it or interacting with it. See if you can temporarily merge with or become it in your attention.

2. Expand to its outer edges.

3. Continue to observe without filters.

4. Notice and affirm: "This is not me. This is something

that I perceive and experience. It is something that I created." Even if you did not create it originally, you are creating and maintaining it for yourself through agreement or acceptance. Notice that this is similar to Dis-Identification.

5. Decide to drop it or let it dissolve.

6. Decide what, if anything, to put into its place by projecting a feeling, intention or affirmation.

7. If there is anything left over, repeat the process on that. If you use a new affirmation and have doubts or disagreement as described above, use the process on that.

TAKING ACTION

1. For the first week or so, just practice basic perception as described above, using the list provided.

2. In the second week, use affirmations to elicit beliefs as described. Also uncover beliefs behind feelings by using "I feel this way because...".

3. For the rest of the month, try using the final process on the material revealed.

NOTES

NOTES

THE CRUCIAL IMPORTANCE OF ETHICS

This lesson deals with ethics and morality, our ideas about right and wrong actions. This is what most people think Karma is all about but they often misunderstand what is happening, thinking that Karma is handing out punishments and rewards. Karma is impersonal. It is not a judge. Things happen simply because other things happened. That being said, our own agency is important in that process and ethics are crucial.

DEFINING ETHICS

Ethics is the branch of philosophy that studies moral judgments and actions, how standards for those judgments and actions are determined and how those standards are organized into systems. These systems and standards are meant to guide us in our choices and behavior with the aim of doing what is best for us and/or others in social interactions.

Our first concern in this lesson will be your own ideas of right and wrong and handling any feelings of guilt or failure that you might hold with regard to living by your own ethics. We will clear up problem areas as best as possible and this will provide great karmic relief for you. Then, we will go deeper into the subject of

Ethics and propose a way to actively use it as a technology for generating good Karma going forward.

HANDLING YOUR ETHICAL KARMA

The following process will help you to clean up ethical problems that you have created over the course of your life. You may find it rough going but it will provide great relief. Fortunately, you have already learned some methods for detachment, increasing willpower and handling emotion and can use these as needed. In working through this process, you will become lighter, spaces will open up and energies will be liberated.

1. Make a list of the moral or ethical qualities that are most important to you.

2. For each one in turn, take a sheet of paper and write the quality at the top. Then, think about your life and list the times that you feel that you came up short in this area. It might help to think back one decade at a time. You absolutely MUST be honest and firm with yourself while doing this and be as thorough as you can. Use as much paper as you need. If it gets ugly for you, just know that you are making changes and persevere.

3. Once that is completely done, repeat the process, listing all of the times that you were strong and good in each area. You must have at least a few examples and probably more than you realized. Let this part of the process show you that you are ethically capable. This will restore you and build up your conviction and strength for the next step.

THE KARMA SUTRA

4. Karma is about action and now you have to take corrective action on the past actions that you have listed. Go through the lists and contact everyone that you acted unethically toward. Maybe there are people that you can not contact or who will not accept contact from you. Just get with who you can and we will address the others later in this lesson.

You should do several things for these people. First, acknowledge what you did wrong and then offer a genuine apology. Most people will appreciate the acknowledgment even more than the apology. Next, suggest ways to repair the relationship and ask what they think would be good, as well. You can certainly work on your acknowledgment, apology and suggestions before communicating with the person but they must be genuine.

It may be hard work but the rewards will be equally great in proportion to your efforts. If it does not work out and the relationship can not be repaired, you tried. It may be a social loss but the karmic relief will still be great.

ANOTHER RITUAL

We mentioned the people that you might not be able to make amends with. Perhaps you do not know how to find them, or perhaps they may not wish to communicate with you or perhaps they might have died in the meanwhile. You can still make a real gesture toward these people by using a variation of the small ritual from Lesson Three involving the glass of water.

After invoking the aid of your Guardian Spirit but before charging and drinking the water, just take the time to acknowledge your actions and make your apologies as you would do in-person and be just as sincere. Next, say something like the following:

"Pull out of our minds, hearts and the karmic web all of the hurtful and unwanted memories, blocks and energies that we have created, accumulated and accepted from the beginning of our creation to the present. Cleanse, purify, sever, cut and release the unwanted or hurtful memories and blocks that tie, bind and attach us together. Let the Water of Life release us all from spiritual, mental, physical, material, financial, and karmic bondage. Cleanse, purify and transmute all these unwanted energies to pure spirit and life energy. Fill the spaces with Divine Will."

Then simply charge and drink the water and finish as before.

ETHICS AS KARMIC TECHNOLOGY

Earlier, we did not suggest types of ethical situations or moral scenarios to help you with the moral inventory that you did but instead encouraged you to consider your own ethical principles. There were two reasons for this.

The first was simply to bring these principles to your conscious awareness. Now that you have listed them, you might want to take some time to think about them. Why are they important to you? When and how did they become important to you? If you have never thought this sort of thing through before, you might go back to the processes in the previous lesson and work with these principles as beliefs or thoughtforms.

This leads into the second reason, which is that your ethical system makes almost NO difference to your karma. Is that a shocking statement? Allow us to explain.

The moral code or set of rules that you try to live by - what you personally consider to be right and wrong - is nowhere near as karmically important as your Consciousness, Responsibility and INTENTION. If you live your life unconsciously, irresponsibly and with intentions that do not resonate with your own true values, you are going to have karmic problems regardless of what your actual system of ethics is.

Probably all of us have encountered a seemingly unethical - even toxic - person that seems to be extremely lucky. This is because people tend to enjoy luck to the same level as their integrity. Wait, what? It may seem strange to say that a toxic person has high integrity, but this can sometimes be literally true in that the person is fairly well-*integrated* as far as their beliefs, values and actions being in harmony.

There are two more Sanskrit terms that are worth introducing here: *phala* and *samskara*. Phala means "fruit" and refers to the explicit fruition or effects of Karma. Samskaras, however, are "impressions" left by psychological experience. They produce our desires and fears which in turn color the impressions of our future experiences. Essentially, samskaras are what we have been talking about all along when we talk about various perceptual filters. How it applies here is the effects that our actions have upon us, regardless of their outer effects on our lives or upon others. We may act against our own ethics and receive an outer gain but we fracture ourselves. Likewise, the moral codes and ethics of others may have nothing at all to do with our own karmic health.

So, with all of that being said, we are going to introduce a simple but powerful ethical code and explain how it may be used as a karmic technology. This is not meant to invalidate your previous ethical principles that you used for your inventory so long as you have examined those principles and hold them consciously. Indeed, invalidation is a major "sin" of the code that we are about to explain.

What we want to propose is a system based simply on a certain kind of respect. It is rooted in Self-respect and its respect for others reciprocally reflects back upon us. It is based on the image of us as those divine sparks, however obscured, but divine nonetheless. This true, essential core nature makes each of us sovereign over our own lives.

The root problem in societies seems to be the lack of real, personal sovereignty. Personal or cultural lack of respect for the sovereignty of Individuals is the foundation for various forms of coercion which allow many forms of abuse to flourish within a society, ranging in scale from dysfunctional relationships and families to general crime to political or religious oppression. These are the conditions that have plagued human societies to a greater or lesser degree throughout history.

As the Russian author Leo Tolstoy put it, "People try to do all sorts of clever and difficult things to improve life instead of doing the simplest, easiest thing - refusing to participate in activities that make life bad."

Respect for the sovereignty of Individuals is expressed in ethics by an axiom or principle that has several names but is best known as the Non-Aggression Principle. According to this principle, aggression is defined as the initiation of force or coercion against another Individual's person or other property. The initiation of force is seen to be a violation of the sovereignty of others.

This is quite simple and should be easily understood. Violent acts, other than those performed in Self-defense (and consensual forms of recreation or sport), are commonly considered to be bad behavior. Taking the property of other Individuals is also looked down upon. Telling other people what they must or must not do is generally perceived as being impolite. And yet, common ethical systems provide loopholes for such behavior which can even become institutionalized. While on the other hand, a society rooted in Individual sovereignty and mutual respect would use an ethical guideline like the Non-Aggression Principle as the basis of all law. In this society, acts such as murder, assault, abduction, theft or destruction of property, fraud and breach of contract would be considered the only crimes. Otherwise, all would be Liberty.

But that is not our immediate concern here. We are interested in what goes on at the fundamental level between Individuals. What we propose is that observing this simple ethical principle continuously re-affirms the divine nature of both ourselves and others but also provides the greatest practical bulwark against social harm. We may be dealing with someone who is absolutely stupid or completely horrible, but we affirm their right to their own karma just as we affirm our own. This can only lead to greater consciousness and responsibility in the long-term while preventing abuse immediately. It should also be noted that the non-initiation of force does not mean that force can not be used in Self-defense. This is not pacifism or passivity (see the final lesson of this course).

Ethical standards are ultimately rooted in *value*. We live by an ethical philosophy because it guides our choices and behavior in ways that steer us toward more of what we value. Because so much of what we value is provided by our exchanges with others, our ethical standards are of crucial importance to sustaining and nourishing our relationships and wider societies. The Non-Aggression principle is an ethical standard that provides the balance between freedom and respect that fully allows our inner divinity and personal sovereignty - which we might consider to be our root values - to flourish into living manifestation.

A SECOND LOOK

So, we ask you to consider this princple and to incorporate it within your ethics if you will. If you do, you can begin to integrate it now by repeating the moral inventory process from the beginning of this lesson with a focus on the following:

1. Acts resulting in the physical harm of another or their property. The primary focus is intentional acts and the initiation of force but unintentional actions may produce a samskara from guilt, so go for both.

2. Invalidating others for their beliefs, opinions, lifestyle choices or general reality. This does not mean disagreement or debate but refers to any denial of the other person's right to make their own choices.

3. Dishonesty. This can be outright lying as well as intentionally misleading or simply withholding information rightful to an interaction. (That last does not mean that you are obligated to reveal all of your and everyone else's secrets, though.)

As before, make amends for these actions. You do not have to repeat anything that you got the first time, of course. Then, simply do your best not to do these things again. In time, you will be transformed, as will your relations with others.

SOME DEEP WORK

When we think about how actions produce effects which produce more actions and effects, on and on without foreseeable stop, it is easy to imagine how our own actions can effect people far beyond us.

Consider that much of the collective problems and suffering of humanity in general are the result of a dense, complex, global web of established and increasing aggression, invalidation and dishonesty. Consider also that this web is woven from the "grassroots" of personal interactions and builds up into larger forms such as war, tyranny and oppression. Consider that suffering exists on this scale because we are all, to some degree, holding each other within it.

This being so, you can extend your work for this lesson (if you wish to do so), by addressing this larger web of karmic effects. You can do this either through the ritual method given above, using an apology for your own part in creating the web and reconciling with everyone affected, or by using the thoughtform dissolving practice from the previous lesson on the web as a whole. Or both!

TAKING ACTION

1. Perform the first moral inventory and begin making amends. The amends may take longer than a month. That is fine, just work steadily at them without slowing down or slacking off. Face-to-face interaction is better than telephone, and telephone is better than a letter or e-mail.

2. After you have begun your amends, perform the second moral inventory on the Non-Aggression Principle and add new amends to your list as necessary. Keep working at them. Begin to practice the Non-Aggression Principle on a daily basis as a CONSCIOUS recognition of the sovereignty and implicit divinity (however obscured) of all people (including yourself).

3. At the end of the month, even if you are still going on with amends, perform the Guardian Spirit ritual and include all people that you can not contact from both inventories as well as the deeper work described above. Alternatively, you may wish to do this as three rituals over as many days as this seems to deepen the experience for some.

4. Finally, you might benefit this month from one more variation of the water ritual. Make a list of everyone who has acted unethically toward YOU - be it by your original standards, the Non-Aggression Principle or through the global web - and state your intent to LET IT GO. This does not mean that what they did was alright. It just means that you are stepping out of the push-pull, cause-and-effect stream of action and reaction. You let it drop and move on consciously and appropriately.

NOTES

NOTES

NOTES

RESOLVING ANCESTRAL KARMA

Much of our circumstance and character, for good or ill, has been shaped by those who have come before us. This is Sabija or Sancita Karma, as described in Lesson One. For those whose family relationships are good, the positive gifts of karmic inheritance can be acknowledged, honored and celebrated. For those whose relationships have not been good, there is understanding and healing to be gained. For most, our family relationships are a mix of the good and the troubled and the work will also be mixed.

YOUR IMMEDIATE ANCESTRAL KARMA

Taking just a page or two for each, consider and write about the following things in the order given:

Who is/was your mother as a person? What is/was her attitude and approach to life? How do you think she feels/felt about her life?

Who is/was your father as a person? What is/was his attitude and approach to life? How do you think he feels/felt about his life?

[If your parents are living, it might be interesting to ask them these things - but do so ONLY after you have recorded and worked with your own impressions of them.]

List the qualities that you like and do not like about

your mother. Which qualities (of both kinds) do you also possess? How do these affect you now?

List the qualities that you like and do not like about your father. Which qualities (of both kinds) do you also possess? How do these affect you now?

Record your answers.

THE KARMIC VALUE OF ANCESTOR VENERATION

Concern with the souls of the dead, particularly the souls of dead family members, is a primal issue in the general context of human spirituality and religion. Veneration of the dead, most especially of the Ancestors, may be the origin of religious belief and practice in general. It has always been an important part of many cultures and religions.

The peoples and cultures that have institutionalized reverence for their Ancestors and honored dead have been primitive and refined, ancient and modern, from all parts of the world. It is actually the cultures that do not engage in this practice today that stand out as unusual.

Like people the world over, you can use a form of veneration to honor your Ancestors and resolve their Karma. The Ancestors lived as all people live. They both experienced and caused their share of wrongs and regrets in life. You can help in healing these conditions. In doing so, you can help the spirits of your Ancestors (if you believe so), perhaps alleviate some of the lingering, present-day effects of these conditions and generally untangle any knots in your family's present Karma. In extreme cases, such entanglements might manifest as a form of "generational curse".

Practical work with the Ancestors begins with setting up a shrine or altar for them. This can be a small, simple space in your home. Traditionally, for concerns of privacy and peaceful sleep, it is generally advised not to set it up in a bedroom. It can be adorned with photographs of deceased Ancestors, objects that belonged to them and items that symbolize your ancestral cultural heritage. Any photographs used should not also contain images of people that are still living and space should be left for making small offerings. These offerings can include food, beverages, incense or candles. The simplest and most essential offerings are candles and water. You will want to do some research and base your offerings on what your Ancestors enjoyed in life and what sort of offerings were culturally traditional for your Ancestors in their own honoring of the deeper Ancestors.

Depending upon your beliefs, such actions may be purely symbolic gestures on your part. That is fine. The deeper regions of the mind are powerfully affected by symbolic action. Whether your approach is spiritual or psychological, these actions will have a beneficial effect on your Karma.

ANOTHER RITUAL

Next, you will want to develop your own ritual for making the offerings. It would be worthwhile to look into the actual cultural traditions of your Ancestors for doing this. However, these need not be followed slavishly and you can also adopt or create other ritual elements. What follows is a general format that covers the basic issues.

THE KARMA SUTRA

First, invoke your Guardian Spirit to facilitate, empower and guide the rite in alignment with your Essential Self, true Life Purpose and Highest Good. "My Guardian Spirit, assist and guide my prayers on behalf of my Ancestors. Align this Work with my Essential Self, my true Life Purpose and the Highest Good for myself and all involved."

Next, call your Ancestors by name. Do the research to get as many names as you can and call them generation by generation back into history. Include those whose names you have not found and ask those called to find and bring the others. Call those who are lost to time and even back through evolutionary history to the Source of Life, if you wish.

Name and present the offerings with something like "To all of those Ancestors that I know and do not know, to all of my Ancestors that I have called and not called, to all of the Ancestors that I remember and do not remember - come and accept these gifts!" Include a second glass of water for use in clearing as you have been doing previously.

As the Ancestors begin to feed, you may make prayers or affirmations for any necessary healing of the Karma of your Ancestral line and for promoting harmony therein.

"Highest of Life, if I, (your name), my family, relatives or Ancestors have offended you or committed any unresolved offense to any other beings in thoughts, words and actions from the beginning of our creation to the present, I humbly ask you and all for forgiveness for all of our errors, resentments, guilts, hatreds, hurts, trauma or pain, offenses, blocks and so forth which we have created and accumulated from the beginning to the present. PLEASE FORGIVE US!

"Let the Water of Life cleanse, purify and release us, offender and offended, from spiritual, mental, financial and karmic bondage. Pull out from our accumulated memory all unwanted, negative memories and blocks that attach, knot, tie and bind us together. Sever, detach, untie and release these unwanted memories and blocks. Transmute these unwanted energies to pure spirit and life energy! Fill the spaces that these energies occupied with Divine Will. Let Right Order, Balance, Understanding, Joy, Wisdom and Abundance be made manifest for us through the power of the Highest of Life, in whom we abide and have our being now and forever more. So be it!"

Then charge and drink the water as usual.

Finally, embrace the Ancestors and ask them to work on your behalf in the realms that they inhabit and with the unique abilities and knowledge that they possess. Ask them to work on your behalf to make you healthy, wealthy and happy, and to keep you so; granting insight, clearing obstacles from your path and bringing good things into your life. Ask that they protect you from harm but also embrace you and guide you in the ways of their realms upon death. Promise them that you will continue to give them nourishment, refreshment and progess.

For those working symbolically, remember that your physical body is literally the accumulated survival wisdom of your Ancestors and that this action still has subconscious power.

How often this ritual is performed is between you and your Ancestors. You may save big offerings and long rituals for special days and simply offer a candle and glass of water each week, using a short and simple version of the ritual. Or, you may go all out each time, making this a central practice in your life. Again, it is up to you and your Ancestors. All families are different. This can only be determined by your own feelings and intuition.

TAKING ACTION

1. In the first week, answer the questions about your mother and father and consider the results. Based on those answers, what portions of this course that you have studied so far are most applicable to those issues? How can you use what you have learned to manage them? Make a plan and do so.

2. In the second week, perform the version of the water ritual given as the final *Taking Action* point in the previous lesson (for letting things go), but now applied specifically to your immediate, living family.

3. In the third week, create a small Ancestor shrine and perform the Ancestor ritual. Record your feelings and experience. Once it is done, do further research both on your Ancestors (genealogy) and your ancestral culture - especially its approach to ancestry. The ritual will open the way to the appropriate information. Modify your ritual accordingly and try it again in the fourth week. Record your feelings and experiences again. Is this a process that you would like to continue?

NOTES

NOTES

WORKING WITH PAST LIVES

This lesson deals with the subject of past lives. Along with the subject of Ethics in Lesson Five, the idea of past lives and reincarnation is the other thing most commonly associated with Karma. There is more than one way to think about this idea and anyone can benefit from working with it, regardless of personal belief system.

REALITY AND RELEVANCE

As with other concepts that we have addressed in this course, you are free to take the concept of past lives either literally or symbolically. Even within this life, you go through a form of reincarnation as you age. You were certainly a very different being when you were developing in the womb, and you "died" from that life to be born into this one. The same is true as you go through transitions from childhood to adolescence, to young adulthood and into maturity. In a sense, you even "die" daily when you go to sleep and are reborn when you awaken.

In any case, for both the believer in reincarnation and the skeptic, ALL memories retrieved in this lesson should be taken as both real and symbolic. Everyone should realize and adopt the position that (a) the memories are real in the sense of being a real communication from your deep mind, but that (b) they may also be symbolic communications like dreams. The memories may or may not be historically real but they will contain relevant information. Whether or not you ever actually lived as Klarkash-ton from Atlantis or as Mary Brown the Victorian governess, the images of Klarkash-ton or Mary and their lives that your mind presents to you will hold some deeper meaning.

EXPLORING YOUR ORIGINS

Taking just a page or two for each, consider and write about the following:

What is your earliest memory? Why do you think that you remember it? What influence or meaning does it have for you now?

What do you know about your own birth? What stories have you heard? What pictures have you seen? How do you think those stories and images have influenced you?

Record the important points and hold on to them for later.

GOING DEEPER

The following regression exercise may help you to obtain glimpses of past lives. Use it with an attitude that is not deadly serious. Approach it as an experiment or game.

1. While lying down or sitting in a comfortable chair, relax and invoke the aid of your Guardian Spirit as in Lesson Three. Ask it to help you to retrieve important

memories that can help you with your present Karma.

2. Make your statement of intent aloud, whether it is to explore a particular issue or simply to open-endedly explore a past life.

3. Deepen your relaxation and go back in your memory to yesterday. Your mind may present something relevant to your statement of intent, as it may for any of the present life steps that follow. Whatever comes up, remember and re-experience that thing from yesterday as fully and vividly as you can.

4. Now go back to last week and remember and re-experience something from that time just as fully and vividly. Repeat this, first going back one month and then one year.

5. Continue going backward and reliving experiences from your past: first a time in your teens, then at about 9 or 10 years old, and finally each year (as best you can) from 5, 4, 3, 2 and 1.

6. Going back even farther, try to remember what it was like to be living in the womb of your mother. Notice whatever sensations, sounds or feelings come to you.

7. Make the decision to go back even further, imagining yourself passing through a light, then look down at your feet.

8. At this stage, notice whatever comes. Look at your body. Explore your surroundings.

9. After just taking that in for awhile, resolve to go to an "important event" either related to an issue that

matters to you now or leaving it open. Experience whatever comes from that life, though you may also ask for a specific message about that life.

10. When you have had enough, slowly and deliberately return to present consciousness and immediately record what you have experienced, including the memories from this life.

IDENTIFICATION WARNING

DO NOT identify with any of these "memories" that you may experience. Remember everything that we have said about identification. If you were advised in Lesson Two not to identify with the beliefs, thoughts, emotions or roles of your CURRENT life, why would it be a good idea to identify with those of a past one? Moreover, if the content of these experiences is only symbolic, as it may well be, then it falls under the same mental phenomena that you were already advised not to identify with. Finally, the whole purpose of this course is to BREAK karmic bonds, not to re-affirm them.

Many people who have powerful experiences of what seems like past life memory can become obsessed with those memories. Do not be one of these people. By all means, learn from your experiences and use what you learn but do not get hung up or stuck.

TAKING ACTION

1. In the first week, answer the questions about your earliest memory and birth and consider the results. Based on those answers, what portions of this course

that you have studied so far are most applicable to those issues? How can you use what you have learned to manage them (if needed)? Make a plan and do so.

2. Over the second and third weeks, try out the regression exercise a few times. Record your results. If the results are spotty, that is fine. Just record them. If you do not have any results at this time, that is fine, too. What portions of this course that you have studied so far are most applicable to what you have uncovered? How can you use what you have learned to manage this material (if needed)? Make a plan and do so. At the very least, include the next two action items.

3. Looking back to the version of the water ritual used in Lesson Five for making amends, repeat that ritual on behalf of any persons that you may have wronged in any and all previous lifetimes. Include anything specific that came up for you in the regression exercise. It would also be beneficial to perform the version where you let go of offenses against you.

4. If material from the regression exercise contains any beliefs, decisions or other thoughtforms that you want to clear, you can use the process from Lesson Four.

5. Again, you need NOT ascribe ANY objective reality to anything that comes up in the regression exercise. You may think of it as purely symbolic. Whether or not you personally believe in reincarnation, the true importance of this information and imagery in either case is PSYCHOLOGICAL. Dis-identfy as needed.

NOTES

NOTES

NOTES

THE CULTIVATION OF DAILY HABITUDE

Our work in this lesson has to do with changing habits. You have probably heard the saying that your beliefs become your thoughts, your thoughts become your words, your words become your actions, your actions become your habits, your habits become your character and your character becomes your destiny. We have written much in this course to explain this process.

In doing so, we have spoken against mechanical behavior and that implies bad things about habit in general. However, while unbroken mindfulness and presence in the moment are promoted as long-range goals in a number of disciplines, we are writing for the average person and not for monks and hermits. Our way is to create relatively immediate benefit by working to turn the habit force back upon itself by replacing unconsciously-acquired habits with consciously-adopted, beneficial ones. Since the habit force exists and is a powerful thing, we want to make it work for us.

HABITUDE

So, what we want to do is to cultivate *habitude* which is a word meaning: the essential character of one's being or existence; native or normal constitution; mental or moral constitution; bodily condition; native temperament.

We have found the core elements of cultivating a beneficial karmic habitude to be Dis-Identification, emotional control, a firm Will and the ethics of the Non-Aggression Principle. Continuing work with the corresponding exercises from Lesson Two and the continuing understanding and application of the Non-Aggression Principle as described in Lesson Five will integrate these perspectives and approaches into your being and make them habitual.

MAKING A COMMITMENT

There is power in decision and commitment. Processes and exercises work but there is something truly magical about the moment that you make a firm decision. It calls a new reality into being and locks it in place. It may take some time for that reality to fully flesh out but we can palpably feel it in the moment of decision.

You could take advantage of this now by making an oath to your Guardian Spirit to live up to the best of yourself and to live ethically. Such an action could generate enormous karmic benefit.

What we propose is invoking your Guardian Spirit as you have done in the past and making an oath like the following:

"I affirm my divine nature and my personal sovereignty in this life. With the help of my Guardian Spirit, I promise and swear that I will forever seek to further discover and live up to the best of my Self in all things. In doing so, I also promise with the help of my Guardian Spirit to recognize and respect the personal sovereignty of each Individual as the exclusive owner of his or her own existence."

You could have this printed in advance and then sign it like a contract. You might then display it somewhere special in your home where you would see it often.

Another good tool is a daily code. You may be familiar with the following one from the Japanese healing system of *Reikido*:

Just for today
Don't get angry
Don't worry
Be grateful
Work hard
Be kind to others.

We might also propose something similar, like the following (with commentary):

Just for today (doable)
Remember who you are (dis-identified, inner divinity, sovereignty)
Be calm (mastering emotion)
Rise to life's occasions (exercising will)
Be respectful and kind to others (non-aggression)
Enjoy and be grateful. (always good)

Again, this is the sort of thing that you might have printed and display in a prominent location. Memorize it, live it, make it habit and your Karma will be changed.

GENERAL ADVICE

There are also a number of smaller (but very powerful) changes that you can make in your daily life that will provide many karmic benefits. Here are a few of the best ones.

1. Decrease your exposure to popular media, especially the so-called "news". Much of popular media is comparable to "junk food" for the mind but the "news" is absolutely toxic. It contains a viciousness and manipulativeness that is pure poison as it bombards you with propaganda (even if it gives you a choice of flavor) and a daily catalogue of tragedies and disasters. By all means, watch shows and films that you truly enjoy, research issues that matter to you but do not spend hours of each day passively letting yourself be filled up with toxins as so many people do.

2. Meditate. It will reduce your stress, improve your concentration and increase your Self-awareness. The most basic form of meditation is to merely be aware of your breathing as you inhale and exhale. Your mind will want to wander but you simply and gently put your attention back onto your breath. If you want something more elaborate, you can think "I" as you inhale and "AM" as you exhale.

3. Do not complain about or criticize situations or people except in the context of constructively seeking or offering a solution. And if it is a solution that you can implement on your own initiative, simply do so.

4. Spend the majority of your time with people who share values, dreams and goals similar to your own. Cultivate those relationships. Minimize relationships and time spent with dysfunctional or negative people.

5. Care for your household. Clear out EVERYTHING that is either unwanted, unneeded or broken. Make a few upgrades. Add entirely new things, including objects that symbolize your spiritual values and goals. Make everything beautiful in its way, even the most mundane or functional things.

6. At the end of each day, recall and review what happened. List everything about the day that was good. Doing this mentally is fine but it is even better to keep small notebooks just for this purpose. Write the date at the top of the page and then list the things. Then, underline each one, saying "Thank you and bless you."

TAKING ACTION

1. Continuing in the practices of this course will make them habitual. While the course, itself, is meant to provide a sort of multi-aspected karmic intervention over the course of nine months (symbolic of gestation and rebirth), many of its processes, exercises and viewpoints can and should be adopted for daily living. This is especially true of Lessons Two and Five (in addition to this lesson and the final one). Moreover, you may wish to repeat the course every few years as a form of karmic hygiene.

2. Invoke your Guardian Spirit and make an oath, using either the one provided or modified as you wish. This

THE KARMA SUTRA

will mark a turning point for you, calling forth a better Self and a better future and making a commitment to them. Remember your oath.

3. Likewise, adopt a code for daily living, using either the one provided or modified as you wish. This will help you to translate your oath into a daily lifestyle. Remember your code.

4. Integrate the General Advice habits into your life. They will go far in helping you to implement your oath and code.

NOTES

NOTES

NOTES

NOTES

MERIT, SERVICE, LUCK AND BLESSINGS

In Buddhism, there is an important and popular idea of making Merit. Merit, in this context, is good Karma. More specifically, though, it is good Karma that dissolves bad Karma - particularly the "soul-harming" kind, as the Jains would put it (Lesson One). It is generated by good thoughts and actions and contributes to the eventuality of spiritual liberation. That can mean for the Individual, for the dead or for all of humanity, as Merit can be ritually transferred or dedicated to others.

The truth is that conscious acts that stop the unconscious, reactive nature of most Karma as well as acts that generate good Karma both produce manifold effects throughout the web of Karma and Merit is actually transferred automatically.

HOW MERIT IS MADE

Here are some traditional examples of how to make Merit:

- giving alms

- observing virtue

- developing concentration

- honoring others

- offering service

- dedicating or transferring Merit to others

- rejoicing in the Merit of others

- listening to Teachings

- instructing others in the Teachings

- straightening one's own views in accord with the Teachings

Some of these have been previously handled in this course - particularly if you think of the course, itself, as a Teaching. The rest are easy to understand, if open to ever-deeper levels of interpretation and application.

We would like to single out one of the methods, offering service, and give it something of a special interpretation and some amplification.

THE BEST FORM OF SERVICE

The best form of service is the service that only you can provide. This is the service that requires you. It requires your specific abilities in your specific time and place.

In the Hindu, Buddhist, Sikh and Jain religions alike, there is this concept of *Dharma* which has a wide variety of meanings and interpretations. The word essentially means to hold, maintain or keep. It refers to what is established and firm and is also often used to refer to law or order. Dharma *sustains*. It can often be used to refer to duty or custom and even ritual. It can mean cosmic or natural law and order as well as referring to a Teaching.

There is a related term, *Svadharma*, that refers to personal Dharma or "own-law", if you like. This is for you and your life what Dharma is to society or the cosmos. It is your particular life path and purpose. Your calling. It is the path you follow toward the highest expression and fulfillment of your own nature. When personal Dharma is accessed, it stands firm, enabling us to act with authenticity from a concentrated state of being.

Of course, there is a strong relation between Dharma and Svadharma. We might think of Dharma primarily as environmental dynamics or the field of existence and Svadharma as the individualized focus. Dharma could be seen as the manifold or context for Svadharma.

KARMA YOGA

Within the Hindu culture, there is an explanation of Karma Yoga or discipline through action to be found within the *Bhagavad Gita* ("Song of the Prosperous"), which is part of the larger epic, *Mahabharata*.

The *Bhagavad Gita* tells the story of two feuding but related clans, the Pandus and the Kurus, who are prepared to meet each other upon a battlefield. With a hundred thousand troops and chariots on each side, they prepared for the mightiest battle yet known to the world. Before the battle, Arjuna, the leader of the Pandus, is deeply troubled because he has friends and relatives on both sides of the bloody conflict that is about to ensue, the battle that he must lead for his side. He receives counsel from his chariot driver, who happens to be the god Krishna.

Before going any further, let us examine the symbolism here. The battlefield is Life, most obviously. Arjuna is the ordinary consciousness of a human and the Pandus are the faculties of consciousness. The war chariot is the body and Krishna is the inner divinity or superconsciousness. The opposing army, the Kurus, are the emotions and identifications of character and personality. So, of course, Arjuna feels affection for the Kurus as his family and companions.

Krishna tells Arjuna that there is no escape from the battle or the battlefield and that he must fight, just as we can not withdraw from existence and must act upon the plane of Life. Arjuna must fight but Krishna advises him to do so with detachment, according to righteous principles and to offer the karmic fruits of his action to Krishna rather than retaining them unto himself.

Alright, let us analyze this. Arjuna, our stand-in, must not fight out of emotion or character attachments. They are the enemy that he is fighting, after all. We covered Detachment in Lesson Two. We also covered Will, which is obviously important here. Arjuna must fight according to righteous principles. We covered our higher meta-needs in Lesson Three, Ethics in Lesson Five and personal Dharma above. That is crucial because our personal Dharma is an expression of our inner divinity, symbolized in this story by Krishna, who explicitly says "Better your own Dharma badly performed than the Dharma of another done perfectly."

The battle, then, is to transform our unconscious, emotionally haphazard actions into actions that express our Dharma in an empowered and ethical way that honors and realizes our inner divinity. This is Karma Yoga.

Now, we are in something of a bind here because full understanding of Dharma is a subject unto itself and beyond the scope of this course - despite being the key to its fulfillment!

However, we can make a very good start. Working through this course will cause you to clarify your being and act with a greater concentration and authenticity as described above. You will begin to ease into your Svadharma and you have the counsel and aid of your Guardian Spirit (Lesson Three), which is our functional image of the inner divinity symbolized as Krishna in the *Bhagavad Gita*. Yes, this is a very good start.

The conscious seal may then be placed upon this Karma Yoga process with the use of a small prayer or affirmation like the following:

"Whatever I perform with my body, speech, mind, limbs, intellect or my inner self, either intentionally or unintentionally, I dedicate it to my Guardian Spirit for my greater understanding. My Guardian Spirit, using my human character as a complementary part and instrument, guides all my actions in alignment with only Divine Will and Purpose."

A word of warning: DO NOT fall into the dangerous trap of identification! This is the invitation to Divinity to act THROUGH the human personality, NOT the elevation of the human personality TO Divinity. Maintain your perspective and remember your ethics. Moreover, this is not a way to shirk accountability. If anything, it is the acceptance of greater responsibility on a deeper level.

HARNESSING THE POWER OF INERTIA

Inertia is something of a dirty word among those of us who value Self-transformation and betterment because it is usually associated with stagnancy. It should be remembered, however, that momentum is also a form of inertia.

Another metaphor, similar to but different from the *Bhagavad Gita*'s chariot metaphor described above, can help to make this understandable. Imagine a man riding an elephant through a jungle. To get where he wants to go, the man must (1) know where he is going and how to get there, and (2) be able to control and guide the elephant. The elephant is much more powerful than the man and does all of the work but the man guides the elephant's power and work to the destination.

The elephant, of course, is the power of inertia - be it in the form of our own habits or within a group. It can either be stubborn and refuse to move or it can take off on a charge that can not be stopped. The man, of course, is the conscious driver - be it in the form of our own reason or a good group leader or manager. All of the ideas, explanations, processes and exercises of the previous lessons in this course are comparable to the training of both the man and the elephant. The elephant is tamed and learns to carry the man and the man learns to assume his place as driver and control the elephant. Personal Dharma is the path or route that the man must know in order to lead the elephant (and be carried by the elephant) to the destination (fulfillment).

HABIT AND LUCK

The force of habit covered in the previous lesson is a form of inertia and it was shown that this force can be turned to our advantage. We can also cultivate habits that help to further turn the inertia of the world to our advantage. Where the former helped us to increase the effectiveness of our regular action, the latter carries into what we might call Luck. In this case, we might use a common definition of Luck as the meeting of preparation and opportunity and then explore how to increase both sides of the equation.

For example, some very general and basic ways to prepare for Luck might include the following:

- carrying a notepad and pen or pencil at all times

- managing your finances efficiently and always having some cash on hand

- cultivating general knowledge

- learning a variety of skills

...while some very general and basic ways to increase your opportunities might be to:

- Cultivate and maintain close relationships with people who share your values, interests and goals. This was mentioned in the previous lesson and a good network is the most important factor in finding opportunities.

- Step off the beaten path. Seek novelty. Explore new ideas and new methods for doing things. Take different routes to and from your job or the grocery store. Spend an evening at a different bar.

- Take advantage of opportunities that present themselves. They will put you in position to access more.

- Be persistent. Do not give up too easily.

Keeping in mind the story of the Chinese farmer and his wise perspective on good and bad fortune, of course, we can certainly make use of such methods to improve our lot even if we face new challenges in the process.

THE GREATER CULTIVATION OF GOOD KARMA

Finally, we can create generating fields beyond ourselves for expressing our Svadharma and for creating good Karma and Merit. We can combine Svadharma with Dharma and dynamic, transforming forces with inertial and manifesting ones. This is like a farmer who acts by planting and cultivating a crop but in partnership with time and the soil. Fields of this type would include our relationships and family, our work and businesses, our educational and charitable groups and other social institutions.

TAKING ACTION

1. Consider the metaphors and symbolism from the *Bhagavad Gita* as well as the elephant metaphor given above. How are they alike? How are they different? Record your thoughts.

2. Use the Karma Yoga affirmation to dedicate your actions to your inner divinity.

3. Experiment with the habits for improving your Luck.

4. Measure your relationships, work and charitable activities against everything that you have learned in this course and your own perspective and feelings as you complete it. What changes would you make in these areas as a way of creating Good Karma or Merit? Record your answers and make the changes.

NOTES

NOTES

NOTES

www.ingramcontent.com/pod-product-compliance
Lightning Source LLC
Chambersburg PA
CBHW020620300426
44113CB00007B/718